"The true power o̲_____ transparency and her dogged persistence in finding answers in the Person and Word of God. Her struggles with identifying God's plan will resonate with every honest seeker. Read this book from cover to cover. Then, keep it handy. You'll want to refer to its reminders again and again."

—Julie-Allyson Leron
speaker, author of 23 books, including
*Sisters in Faith Bible Study* series and *Praying Like Jesus*
www.joymediaservices.com

"Finally, a book that confronts a tough issue! This book helps us examine our concepts of prayer and our responses when life gets messy."

—Linda Hardin
single adult and women's ministries coordinator,
Church of the Nazarene

"As an advocate for breast cancer patients, I meet many people who struggle with questions about the will of God. This book is a must read; not only for the method it teaches, but for the message of hope—positive hope—it delivers."

—Deb Haggerty
writer, speaker, breast cancer survivor
www.positivehope.com

"Cheri's ideas, inspiring stories, and challenging questions are valuable resources for readers interested in making important life decisions. Do yourself a favor by preparing now for the time when you will be asking, "What does God want me to do?"

—Burrell D. Dinkins
professor, Asbury Theological Seminary,
author of *Narrative Pastoral Counseling*

"This book is beautifully written, deeply spiritual, wonderfully personal, and remarkably helpful. Read it and pass it on to those you love most."

—Robert Tuttle Jr.
professor, Asbury Theological Seminary,
author of *Sanctity Without Starch:
A Layperson's Guide to a Wesleyan Theology of Grace*

# DIRECTION

A COMPANION WORKBOOK FOR PRACTICING THE PROCESS OF DISCERNMENT

# DIRECTION

## »CHERI COWELL«

**DISCERNMENT FOR THE DECISIONS OF YOUR LIFE**

Pleasant Word
A Division of WINEPRESS PUBLISHING

Pleasant Word (a division of WinePress Publishing,
PO Box 428, Enumclaw, WA 98022) functions only as
book publisher. As such, the ultimate design, content,
editorial accuracy, and views expressed or implied in
this work are those of the author.

ISBN 13: 978-1-4141-1046-2
ISBN 10: 1-4141-1046-4
Library of Congress Catalog Card Number: 2007904513

# CONTENTS

# INTRODUCTION
## HOW TO USE THIS BOOK

It's a joke with family and friends that I wrote a book titled *Direction*, for if you should turn me around three times I wouldn't be able to find my way out of a paper bag. I'm not too good with north and south. I'm better with left and right, and best with, "Turn at the house with the purple mailbox and a bush shaped like a dinosaur." Fortunately for you, this isn't a book on reading a map or finding your way around town, although I am using a few "directional signs" to help guide you through the lessons. And although I don't claim to be an expert at spiritual discernment and decision-making, I have studied in this area for some time. I'm praying that my mistakes and experiences while searching for answers will help smooth your path. So, before we begin, here are a few tips for getting the most out of this journey.

This companion workbook is designed to be used in tandem with the book *Direction: Discernment for the Decisions of Your Life* (Beacon Hill, 2007), and is designed to deepen your faith-walk and help you *apply* what the book teaches. This workbook is divided into two parts: the group lessons, which begin with an introductory class, and the weekly lessons designed for the individual. The weekly lessons begin with Chapter One of the book, but assume you've read the introductory chapter. Although you may choose to use this workbook as an individual study, I encourage you to find a few people to join you in the journey because so much of what we learn, we learn through the relationships we build.

Here is a layout of the group and individual lessons:

- Introductory group class (participants may or may not have read the introductory chapter before this meeting)
- Weekly lessons, followed by a weekly group gathering covering each chapter, one through eight

Ideally, the group lessons would follow the weekly lessons, but can also fall somewhere *during* that week, as scheduling permits. The weekly lessons should take twenty to thirty minutes and follow the reading of the book. A Bible, pen, and this workbook are all that's needed. Access to the Internet is a plus, as several times you may be directed to a Web site for more information, but it isn't necessary. If you're leading the group sessions, see "Notes for Group Leaders" for a list of things you'll need. Participants in those sessions will only need a pen or pencil for notes, this workbook, and their Bibles. The group lessons are designed to be completed within forty-five minutes to an hour.

A note on the "direction signs" used in this study: These headings are meant to guide you as you journey through each lesson. Just as you recognize a road sign on the highway and are alerted to what lies ahead, these "signs" are to inform you of the purpose of each part of the lesson. Below is a key that will help you navigate these signs. Like road signs, after a few lessons, they should become second nature.

- Stop: This tells you to stop and look up a passage in your Bible.
- Intersection: This sign indicates an "intersection" with the book *Direction*.
- Discern: Imagine a road sign with a question mark. This is a place for pondering.
- Direction: This is a heads-up, pay-attention place—a yellow highlighter indicator.
- Decision: This is an opportunity to practice decision-making.
- Yield: This is a call to prayer.

## Notes For Group Leaders

Whether you're a seasoned group leader or this is your first opportunity to lead a small group, welcome! I want you to know how privileged I am to be taking this journey with you. For, as I wrote this workbook, I thought about you and prayed for you. You are vital to the church and to the family of God. I am excited for you because I know the leader always receives more from the study than anyone else in the class. To teach is to really understand, and to teach a Bible study means we must get inside what we're learning—trying out all the angles, exploring all of the questions—and then allowing the message to sink in and transform us.

First, let me remind you that you are not alone. In fact, the Holy Spirit is the teacher of this class and you're simply the assistant who makes the path smooth for the Spirit to do His work. Second, there is no perfect or right way to lead these lessons. Don't get too wrapped up in trying to "get it right." Your class members are grateful for your leadership (most appreciate whatever you do because they can't imagine doing what you're doing). Finally, regardless of what you choose to do to prepare, the most important thing you can do is to pray. Pray for the presence of the Holy Spirit in your class, pray for the people who are being drawn to take this class, and then pray for each member by name each week as you study and grow together. Pray that God will guide the group discussions and will minister to the individual needs, both those known to you and the unknown. Then pray that God will make *Himself* known through this study, that He will be glorified in all you say and do. If you do this, I know God will bless your time together and make it a sweet and lasting experience for you and your group members.

A note about the structure of the lessons: Each group lesson, although slightly different each week, follows the same basic format.

- Gathering Activity—this is an activity that will need preparation (see the "Resources Needed" list).

- Opening Prayer—you may read or invite others to share in this reading.

- Weekly Review—this is where you will discuss the weekday lessons the class members did on their own. You will use the questions to guide the discussion. Remember, not all questions need to have answers.

- Next is the main part of the lesson, and it changes from week to week.

- Most lessons end with a time of prayer (Yield), although some end with other prayerful activities.

A note about preparation and the resources needed: It's important that you carefully review each lesson before the meeting, making certain you understand each activity and the flow of the meeting. There are a variety of approaches to the lessons, some you may be more excited about and comfortable with than others. Feel free to enlist the help of someone in your group for those parts of the lesson you're less at ease with. For instance, you may not be a drama person but know someone in the group who is outgoing and would be less intimidated. Ask them to help you with that part. Don't hesitate to enlist the gifts of others.

In Appendix C, there's a list—"Resources Needed for Each Group Lesson." This is a great place to start as you review the upcoming lesson. You'll also find a goldmine of resources at my Web site, www.directionanddiscernment.com, including church bulletin inserts and posters for publicity, signs for your classroom door, and downloadable PDFs for specific lessons.

Please feel free to contact me through my Web site with questions and feedback. I'd love to hear what you're doing and how this study has impacted your life. You may also want to take pictures and add them to the photo gallery. It is so much fun to see the creativity of God at work in His people. But most of all, I'd love to pray for you. Through my Web site you can send the time and dates of your class, and I will pray for you specifically. May God's richest blessings be yours as you seek to serve the One who gives us all we ever need and more.

And now…let the journey begin.

# INTRODUCTORY GROUP LESSON

**G**athering Activity: BEFORE the meeting, be sure to have enough nametags, Bibles, and pencils for those coming. Place a basket of oranges and/ or apples on a center table along with a sign which reads "Jeremiah 17:7-8." Also, you'll need pieces of paper with the name of one of four kinds of fruit —apples, oranges, grapes, peaches. As each person enters, have them get a nametag and a slip of paper with their favorite fruit. You may need to participate to accomplish an even number.

**Opening Prayer:** Dear God, we're grateful to be gathered here in your name, for the opportunity to learn more about You, and to grow in our faith. As we study together, help us to truly meet each other, getting to know one another beyond the surface. And in that knowing, may each of us find love, acceptance, and grace. We ask this in the name of the One who is Grace. Amen.

**Weekly Review:** As the leader, share how this study is structured. Explain the weekly self-studies that follow the book chapters. Explain that a chapter will be read in the book each week along with the corresponding Bible study workbook pages. Be sure they know if they fall behind in their reading, they should still come to the group gathering, as their presence is important to the group. Explain that some may have already read the introductory chapter in the book, and that is okay. Next week, if they haven't already, they'll want to read the introductory chapter *plus* the first chapter and the week's lessons. This is the only week when they'll need to double up on their reading. Each weekday lesson in this workbook is designed to be completed in twenty to thirty minutes, and is designed to be done in tandem with the book reading. The group lessons are intended to last forty-five minutes to an hour.

**Reading:** Read aloud the section subtitled "Show Me The Way" in the "Introductory Chapter."

**Discussion Questions:**

1. Who is the person or persons in your life from whom you learned how to live as a Christian?

2. Who was your model for the method you now use when determining God's will?

3. Of the four guideposts listed, which one do you rely on the most when determining God's ways?

4. Which one, if any, do you have more difficulty in applying?

**Reading:** Continue reading from the introductory chapter under the heading, "The Personal Pathways Approach."

**Group Exercise:** Say: The next set of questions will be answered by playing that favorite old-time game "Fruit Basket Toss Up." I'll read the question slowly, and then the name of a fruit (or fruits). All those with that fruit name on their slip of paper must stand up and switch seats with another person who is also standing. The last person to sit must answer the question. There is one instance when everyone will stand and switch seats, and that's when I say, "Fruit basket toss up." Again, the last person to sit must answer the question. (Note: for those with physical limitations, this game can be changed by laying a hula hoop on the floor in the center of your room and handing a beanbag to each person. When their fruit name is called, they'll toss their beanbag into the hoop. The person the farthest from center must answer the question.)

## Questions for Fruit Basket Toss Up

- Do you believe the Bible teaches that God has ordained a personal plan for your life for you to find?

- Do you agree or disagree with the author that the Personal Pathways Approach leaves you with more questions than answers?

- I have tried some or all of these guideposts for discerning God's will with similar results as the author. True or false?

- I have often feared that because these methods didn't work for me, there might be something lacking in my faith. True or false?

- I believe that prayer should be our primary means for discerning God's will. True or false?

- I believe the agreement of signs—the open and closed door and counsel of the wise—is a good way to make good decisions. True or false?

- I believe the Bible contains all we need to make wise and godly decisions. True or false?

- I rely heavily on the inner peace of the Holy Spirit to guide me in my decision-making. True or false?

**Stop:** Pass out Bibles and have everyone look up Jeremiah 17:7-8. Read it aloud, and compare any different translations. Explain that this is the memory verse for this class. By the end of the eight weeks, you hope they can have it memorized. You may want to pass out index cards for each person so they can write out the verse. Tell the group this verse explains what the author hopes each person will experience by the end of the class—confidence in the Lord, knowing how God communicates His will to His people, and bearing the fruit of a well-rooted tree.

**Yield:** Close your time together by joining hands or placing your hand on each other's shoulder. Pray that God would honor your time in study by making it sacred. Invite God to speak to each person this week in a unique and personal way, and ask that you are brought back together again next week, eager to grow and learn.

**Directional "*signs*" in my week**

*Day One*

**Direction:** The first question asks, "Is it _____ with the _____ of God?"

**Stop:** Read 2 Samuel 11:2-27

**Discern:** Look at this list of God's character qualities. Add to the list any qualities you've known God to manifest. Circle those qualities you consider to be your strengths and place a box around those you consider to be your areas of weakness.

### God's Character Qualities

| | | |
|---|---|---|
| Loyal | Righteous | Loving |
| Trustworthy | Holy | Yielded |
| Honest | Self-controlled | Compassionate |

**Decision:** Instead of focusing on your weaknesses and trying to fix them, what does 2 Corinthians 12:8-9 say you should do with them?

**Yield:** In prayer, thank God for endowing you with parts of His character—the strengths you've circled. As you focus on shining forth in your strengths, invite God to enter into the weaknesses you've identified, weaknesses that only *with* and *in* His power can they become strengths. Praise Him that in your weaknesses, He is strong.

*Day Two*

**Intersection:** What are the three reasons we must ask the first question: _____,_____, _____ (pg. 32-36)?

**Decision:** In reading the stories of Bonnie, Connie, and Vanessa, for which person do you find the most compassion? Which "need" might this reveal in your own life?

**Stop:** Read Exodus 16:15-20. What do the Scriptures tell us was the result of measuring the manna (bread from heaven)? What happened to the bread of those who gathered more than they could eat before morning?

**Direction:** As the saying goes, if our _____ is propped up against the _____ wall, climbing to the _____ won't get us _____ we _____ (pg. 37).

**Discern:** There are several reasons for a distorted or inaccurate view of God. Check those that apply to you.

_____ suffered emotional, physical, or sexual abuse as a child/teenager

_____ raised in an overly strict household

_____ experienced extreme suffering for which you were not to blame

_____ what the author calls "our pluralistic society"

_____ unfamiliarity with the person of God

_____ other _____

**Stop:** Read John 6:48-51

**Yield:** In prayer, praise God for the Living Bread He has supplied in the sacrificed body of His only Son. Thank Him that in this Bread of Heaven, all your needs are met. Finally, ask Him to help you untangle the distortions you may have of Him, and to reveal Himself to you fully and completely through this study.

*Day Three*

**Stop:** Read Exodus 3:13-15. What is God's name and what do the Scriptures say it means?

**Discern:** Are you familiar with what your name means? Is there a "story" behind the giving of your name? The names you gave your children? Your mother or father's name?

**Decision:** What does it mean for you to call God your "Father," or "Abba, Daddy" (pg. 39)?

**Intersection:** Look through the "Names of God List" in the book's index and do a search or study of the name you're drawn to most. For a list of resources, and to receive a "top ten list" of the author's favorite names of God along with a free prayer card, go to www.directionanddiscernment.com.

**Yield:** As you pray this week, use the personal name of God you researched or the intimate "Abba, Father." Imagine not only talking to the Great Creator God, but also to your Abba, Father—your Daddy.

*Day Four*

**Stop:** Read Luke 15:11-24

**Discern:** List the gifts you've been given as part of your inheritance as a son or daughter of Christ the King. Be sure to not only list your personal gifts, but also those things you share as a member of God's family and as a member of creation.

<u>**My Inheritance in Christ**</u>

**Intersection:** The term *prodigal* means recklessly wasteful; to squander. In what ways has humanity been recklessly wasteful with our inheritance from our Heavenly Father?

**Decision:** All of us have wasted time, resources, and opportunities. In what ways have you personally squandered your inheritance?

**Direction:** When we make a_____, either unwittingly or deliberately, He can use that to_____ who He is and _____ to be (pg. 39).

**Yield:** In prayer, ask God to forgive you and your fellow citizens for the reckless wastefulness of the good things He meant for our blessing. Be specific. Now, like the prodigal son or daughter, come to your Father with humility, seeking God's forgiveness for squandering your inheritance. Then imagine your heavenly Father running to meet you, wrapping you in His arms and saying, "All is forgiven, for what was lost now has been found."

*Day Five*

**Intersection:** What are your earliest memories of hearing about God? How was God presented? Was God more of a...

_____ distant being?

_____ close companion or friend?

_____ overbearing and rigid ruler?

**Discern:** Do you find it easier to relate to God with reverence and awe, or as Best Friend (pg. 40)?

**Stop:** Read John 15:1-8. Who is the vine? _____ Who is the gardener? _____ Who are the branches? _____
What are the two roles of the Gardener? He _____ branches that do not bear fruit, and _____ branches that do bear fruit.

**Decision:** The word _remain_ or _abide_ is used _____ times in these verses. Verse 7 tells us that remaining in Jesus Christ means abiding in and staying connected to His Word. In what ways do you need to adjust your life so as to abide more closely in or stay connected to Jesus?

What is the result of staying grafted in Christ, the True Vine?

**Direction:** We will bear the fruit of _____ decision-making when we are _____ to the _____ and _____ our relationship with _____ as our _____ (pg. 41).

6

**Yield:** Share with God your desire to be fully and completely grafted in Him and to know Him as intimately as a Best Friend. Ask God to help you adjust your behavior in accordance with His likes and dislikes, pruning where He sees need so as to produce in you a pleasing, fruit-bearing branch.

## GROUP STUDY
## LESSON ONE

**Gathering Activity:** Before the meeting, create nametags (or download them from www.directionanddiscernment.com) that read, "I see God as..." When group members arrive, have them fill in the blank on their nametag with Father, Guide, or Friend. As they mingle, invite them to share why they made that choice and, if they feel comfortable, their earliest impressions of God.

**Opening Prayer:** Father God, we thank you for bringing us together and for giving us the opportunity to learn more about you through the gift of community. Guide us as we open the Scriptures together, and speak to each of us by using this study, our discussion, and your Holy Spirit. May we come to know you more intimately over this next hour. We come to you, our Abba, in whose Holy name we pray. Amen.

**Weekly Review:** Discuss the week's lessons. What stood out for you in the reading or study? What questions did it create? What did you struggle with the most?

**Reading:** Reread "The Rest of the Story" near the end of Chapter One (pg. 43).

**Discussion Questions:**

1. Which is more difficult for you to accept: God's action in taking David's son's life despite David's pleas, or David's acceptance and about-face after his son's death?

2. The reading refers to David having had two choices: hold onto his pain and hold _____ accountable, or let go of his _____ and trust God (pg. 45).

**Read**: 2 Samuel 12:1-14

Often it's easier to see sin for what it is when we see it in someone else's life. Had Nathan accused David directly about his sins, David probably would have denied and defended. Instead God allowed David to see his sin in someone else. God uses many tools to confront us, to redirect us, and to send us in the right direction. Together, make a list of the many and varied ways God gives us direction.

**Read**: 2 Samuel 12:15-24. Note in verse 13 that David sought God's forgiveness and it was given. What was the penalty David might have suffered had he not asked for forgiveness?

David confessed and was forgiven—sparing his life, but the consequences of his sin were irreversible. David's son hadn't sinned and yet suffered the consequence of his father's sin. Forgiveness and suffering the consequences of that sin are two different things.

Forgiveness allows communion with a loving and Holy God, but it doesn't erase consequences. God's character dictates how the world, which He created, is to operate. When the created (all of humanity) violate the principles of His character, we must suffer the consequences.

**Direction:** Therefore, it's important for us to ask the first question, "Is it _____ with the _____ of _____?" Doing so helps us to identify ways God might be confronting, redirecting, or sending us in the right direction.

**Small Group Sharing:** If your group is large, divide into groups of three or four. As a small group, look at the list of God's character qualities in the index. Discuss which of these character qualities David violated. Which are more easily violated? Which are easiest for you to conform to?

Often we must fall into a pit before we come face-to-face with who we are apart from God. David came to that point while keeping vigil at his son's bedside. Think about a time when you've had to face your own sinfulness in light of God's goodness. Perhaps you are there now. Share with the group, as you feel comfortable. Then close your time together by using Psalm 51 (a plea for mercy) or Psalm 32 (a praise for God's faithfulness), whichever seems most appropriate for your group, as a closing prayer.

**Directional "*signs*" in my week**

*Day One*

**Direction:** The second question asks, "Is there an
_____ or _____?"

**Discern:** Mark all of the phrases you have used
or have heard others use when confronted with
unexplained suffering.

_____ God never gives us more than we can
handle.

_____ God must have something wonderful planned
if He is allowing this much suffering.

_____ It's probably for the best.

_____ Things could have been worse.

_____ You know, God is in control.

_____ God must have His reasons.

_____ God must be trying to teach you/us
something.

**Direction:** There are two things people facing obstacles and opposition need from you and me—acknowledgement of their feelings, and compassion. The following list is an alternative to the commonly used phrases listed above. Look through the list and choose one or two from each area that you intend to use the next time someone needs words of comfort and compassion.

*Acknowledge their feelings:* This must be very hard for you. I wish I could take away the hurt. I cannot imagine your pain, but I'm here for you. I'm sorry—I know how much you loved him/her.

*Offer compassion:* I'm praying for you. Please know I am here for you. I don't know why this happened, but I'm here to share your pain. I can't undo what has happened, but I can sit with you as you grieve.

**Intersection:** How we see God's _____ in our suffering _____ how we seek His _____ (pg. 50).

**Yield:** In prayer, ask God to help you represent His love and compassion when others are hurting. Ask Him to open your eyes and heart to see and feel their pain so that you can acknowledge their feelings without judgment. Then, with your heart made tender, invite God to pour out His compassion through the words you share.

*Day Two*

**Intersection:** The first of three faulty views of God that color how we seek His leading is _____ doesn't want me to _____ (pg. 50).

The author gives three reasons for this faulty view:
a religiously _____ household,
an _____ home,
or a _____ figurehead (parent or religious leader).

**Discern:** Said another way, would you say you view God more like a stern, unbending Judge_____, or a loving and joyous Creator _____?

**Direction:** This view of God tends to create in us a fear of choosing a path that might bring joy or happiness. On the contrary, people who hold this view believe Christians are *supposed* to suffer, almost wearing their sufferings like badges of honor. Do you find it hard to believe the author's premise that God *never* intended His children to suffer?

**Stop:** Read Luke 19:11-27

**Decision:** Often it is simply our natural personality or bent that causes us to be cautious. Being careful and cautious are both good qualities, but when our natural personality combines with a faulty, fearful view of God, those good qualities can become anchors to our faith. If you're naturally cautious— always counting the cost before moving forward, even cautious to an extreme—*and* you've recognized yourself in the above described view, take some time to review the personality resources listed in the index and at www.directionanddiscernment.com. There you'll also find a list of books about the love and joy of God, a concept that may need to "grow on you" and merge with a fresh understanding of how God created you, personality and all.

**Yield:** Praise God for the life you've been given. If you were led to believe this faulty view of God by someone of authority in your life, offer that person or people forgiveness. Then ask God to help you learn to see Him as loving and joyful, desiring you to be joy-filled and happy.

*Day Three*

**Intersection:** The second faulty view is that _____ is _____ me (pg. 52). Can you recall a time in your life when it felt as though God were punishing you? The author tells us there are two things at the heart of this view: a picture of God as _____ and as vengeful (pg. 53). Do you believe God gets angry? Is He vengeful?

**Stop:** Read Job 1:6-22, 2:1-10

**Discern:** Although we're told why Job is suffering, Job did not know. Yet, what does verse 1:20 say Job did?

After Job lost his possessions, his children, and his health, it is understandable why his wife would be disgusted at Job's lack of anger. Although God later chides Job for his answer to her, what is the basis for Job's belief about his suffering (see verse 2:10)?

**Stop:** Read Job 40:1-14, 42:1-17

**Decision:** Throughout Job's ordeal he made it clear that all he wanted was to plead his case before God. When God finally gives Job that chance, he falls silent. Why? When bad things happen to you, do you demand to know why?

God goes on to answer the heart of Job's question, which doesn't ask why he's suffering, but how God would do that to him (verse 2:10). When finally confronted with the goodness and justice of God, Job recognizes that his plea for "fair treatment" has been heard, even though God does not tell him the "whys" of his situation. In the end, Job speaks (42:1-6). In light of God's sovereignty, goodness, and mercy, Job does the only thing he can: he seeks God's forgiveness for questioning His character. Have you questioned God's goodness in the midst of your own suffering? God is ready and willing to answer our deepest questions of faith, but the story of Job is a warning against questioning God's goodness and faithfulness.

**Yield:** In prayer, ask God to forgive you for your lack of trust in His power and love. Just as Job did, admit to Him your limited vision and lay yourself at His mercy. Then sit in silence, allowing God to demonstrate that great mercy and love.

*Day Four*

**Intersection:** View three is: God has _____ it and someday I'll _____ (pg. 56).

**Stop:** Read Genesis 1:26-27

**Discern:** In what ways are we "made in God's image"? How are we different from God?

<u>Made in God's Image</u>    <u>Different from God</u>

**Stop:** Read Genesis 2:15-17

**Intersection:** Using verses 1:26 and 2:15, write your understanding of what the author calls "the gift of free-will and the role of co-creators in apprenticeship with God" (pg. 57).

If creative freedom is the _____ of our God-image, then _____ is our trademark, our lasting _____ designating us as God's true image bearers (pg. 57).

**Discern:** The concept of *shalom* at its root means wholeness, safety, perfect peace, or unity and harmony. This is what we were created for—to live in harmony with God and all He created. How does this "longing for peace" relate to our desire for fairness and justice when we encounter obstacles and opposition?

The biblical vision of *shalom*, Bishop John Taylor (English Priest and theologian –1914-2001) writes, "meant a dancing kind of inter-relationship, seeking something more free than equality, more generous than equity."[i] The author of *Direction* says (pg. 58) that "living in tension" between this sin-soaked world and the state of shalom we're being returned to by the work begun in us by the life, death, and resurrection of Christ, is also called the "already-not-yet theology." How are we "already" being returned to shalom (see the definition of shalom above), and how are we "not yet" there?

[i] John Taylor, Enough is Enough (Minneapolis, Minn.: Augsburg Publishing, 1977), 42.

How then is suffering a violation of God's plan?

How does this understanding of suffering change your view of God?

**Yield:** Thank God for His gift of shalom, the Prince of Peace—His only Son—whom He sent in order to return us to that state of wholeness and harmony we were created for but lost because of our sin. Thank Him for His grace and mercy that while we were yet sinners He created a way for us to return to that peace. Ask God to help you embrace your role as co-creator, that while living in the "already-not-yet," you may be an instrument of peace in His hand.

*Day Five*

**Stop:** Read John 14:9-11

**Direction:** To know God's response to our suffering, we need look no farther than _____ (pg. 59).

**Stop:** Read Mark 1:40-42

What things in our society make someone "untouchable"?

In your own life, are there things that make you *feel* unclean?

What would it mean if Jesus were to touch you with His healing hand?

**Stop:** Read John 9:1-11

Like the disciples, when confronted with unexplainable suffering, we often look for someone or something to blame. Rather than looking for blame, what does verse 4 say we are to do?

**Intersection:** The first thing God does in response to our suffering is He is _____ with us. Just like Solomon Rosenberg's wife, God also _____ us into our _____ sufferings. Finally, God, with righteous anger at the _____ He sees, reaches out to _____ us where we most need it (pg. 61).

**Yield:** In prayer, picture yourself before God, holding all those things that make or have made you feel unclean. Look into God's eyes as He has compassion on you and watch the pain you've experienced show on His face. Now allow God to take those painful, shame-producing things from you, and feel His healing touch as He whispers the words, "You are now clean."

GROUP STUDY
LESSON TWO

**Gathering Activity:** As people gather, invite them to help prepare for the "dramatic reading" that will be a part of the lesson. Have the props, costume pieces, and scripts available and have the group choose parts, set the scene, and dress the actors.

### Casting/Costumes/Props

- A solid color bathrobe or a sheet with rope-belt, for *God*
- A sheet wrapped toga-style for *Habakkuk*
- A hat or sunglasses to designate the *Narrator* (who will read the "Background Information" and the beginnings of Habakkuk 1:1, 2:2, and 3:1, which are clearly not dialogue)

**Props:** A sheet of paper rolled like a scroll and a feather pen (in Habakkuk 2:2 the Lord tells Habakkuk to write down what He is saying, Habakkuk writes as the Lord speaks, and then reads his writing, which is his prayer in 3:2-19).

**Opening Prayer:** God of love and compassion, thank you for hearing our cries for help when we feel persecuted and unfairly attacked. Please forgive us for questioning your goodness, and help us to respond to the suffering surrounding us, not by pointing fingers and looking for blame, but instead with the same mercy and love you've shown us.

Speak to us through this study. May we learn to respond to suffering—ours and the suffering of others—as you would have us. In the name of the One who heals. Amen.

**Weekly Review:** Discuss the week's lessons. What stood out for you in the reading or study? What questions did it create? What did you struggle with the most?

**Background Information:** Habakkuk lived in Judah during the reign of Jehoiakim (juh hoi uh kim), the fourth wicked king to serve the Southern kingdom, a king who oppressed his people and rejected God. The Babylonians were sitting on the outskirts of Judah, threatening to invade (an invasion that would occur shortly after this writing). It appeared that evil men were winning, that good men and women were needlessly suffering, and, even worse, that God was nowhere to be found.

**Drama:** Use a Bible translation that allows for easy reading of Habakkuk. NIV, NRSV, NLT are a few good translations for this purpose.

**Discussion Questions:**

1. In what ways are Habakkuk's questions similar to ours today?
2. Habakkuk had trouble squaring the injustice and suffering he saw with who he knew God to be—sovereign and good. What is God's answer to Habakkuk's questions?

**Small Group Sharing:** If your group is large, divide into groups of three or four. As a small group, discuss the *lie*—the concept of the Path of _____(pg. 62), and the *truth*_____and _____ are a part of the life we must live in the _____ of the _____-_____-_____ (pg. 64). Share, as you feel comfortable, your own struggles in holding onto this truth and rejecting the lie. Close your time together by reading 1 Peter 2:19-21 (pg. 66) as your prayer.

# WEEK THREE

**Directional "*signs*" in my week**

*Day One*

Stop: Read Psalm 104:1-4
Make a list of where you see the evidence of God.

## I See God...

Intersection: After reading the author's description of the "deep hole" or "dark prison" where God seems very distant (pg. 68), list situations in your own life where her description would be a fitting analogy of yours.

Discern: The term "blind faith" is almost a slur when used by non-Christians to describe the Christian's belief in God and His Son, Jesus Christ. Likewise, when someone does something he or she cannot fathom doing, they often attribute that person's steps of faith to "blind faith" (pg. 69). What do you think they might mean by using that term?

**Stop:** Read 2 Peter 1:12-21

**Direction:** Our faith is made possible by the work of the Holy Spirit working in our hearts and minds, showing us the truth of God in Scripture, and in the evidence that surrounds us. The Holy Spirit then enables our steps of faith, teaches us what we are to know, and reminds us of those truths when our faith grows weak. Sometimes the Holy Spirit uses Scripture, sometimes it is men and women of faith, and other times it can be the things of this world. In what ways does the Holy One give, restore, and grow *your* faith?

**Yield:** In prayer, thank God for the gift of faith, and ask Him to forgive you for the times you may have accepted it as a work of your own. Invite the Holy Spirit to show you facets of faith you have yet to see, and then ask for the courage to step out in that faith as a witness to His grace.

*Day Two*

**Intersection:** Two snares are hidden along *Too Small Trail.*

The first one is a vice-turned-virtue that has several names (pg. 71). List them here.

The second snare, a closely related cousin, is our need for _____. And it shares the same root of _____ from the family tree.

**Stop:** Read Matthew 4:1-11

**Discern:** Applying the Too Small analogy, how does Satan try to trap Jesus into thinking His God is too small, powerless, or weak (pg. 72)?

How does Satan tempt you into believing God is too small?

The author tells us that when we hear Satan whisper these lies, we are to respond as Jesus did. How did Jesus respond to Satan's temptations?

Satan's snares can place us in a black hole where truth and light are hard to see. The temptation of Christ tells us that Satan is a crafty one, but one who can be turned away with truth. When we know the truth of God's Word, Satan is revealed as the truly small, weak, and powerless one. Our God is not too small!

**Yield:** In prayer, ask God to uproot the pride in your heart that allows you to be trapped by Satan's lies. Ask Him to forgive your desire to control things, to believe that you might be independent and self-reliant. Then ask Him to forgive you for allowing your need for security to become an idol. Finally, praise Him for being a great and mighty God, a God who protects you from the "evil one" and will safely see you back down the mountain and into His arms.

*Day Three*

**Intersection:** The first snare on *Too Big Trail* is that God is too big to _____. When our God is "too big," He becomes _____ and _____ (pg. 73).

The other closely related snare is the division of the _____ and the _____.

In what ways have you succumbed to either of these snares (pg. 74)?

**Direction:** The truth is, our God is just big enough to care about the little things of life. What are some little things you haven't prayed about that you now wish to bring before the Lord?

**Stop:** Look at 1 Kings, Chapter 8:22-54. Solomon, the wisest king to rule over Israel, prays a prayer of dedication over the newly built Temple. Notice in verses 27-30 and in verses 31-51 the places where the word *when* is used. Solomon lists the many instances when God's people will come before Him in prayer. Note how varied these instances are—some are big things and some are small—and yet Solomon, in speaking before the whole assembly of Israel, tells God His people will bring their prayers for these things and more. We recognize these were simply types or examples of the prayers to be brought before the Lord, not an exhaustive list. Now read verses 52-54 where Solomon asks God to receive these prayers as earnest pleas to a God who is faithful to hear them *and* to answer them because of who God is.

**Yield:** As Solomon did, open your prayer time pleading for mercy, and ask God to hear your prayers no matter how small they are. As you do, acknowledge Him as a God who is not too big to care about the little things in your life. Now close your prayer as Solomon did, thanking God for His abiding nearness and faithfulness in hearing your prayers. Thank Him for the truth that nothing is ever off-limits; nothing is too earthly for His concern.

*Day Four*

**Intersection:** In reading the author's explanation of the different stances Christians take when it comes to God's sovereignty (pg. 75-76), where would you place yourself on this continuum?

**(Sovereign)**                        **(Limited Sovereignty)**

---

| Absolute * | Control with | * Control + Freedom * | Absolute |
| Control | Some Freedom | | Freedom |

This subject is one that divides, and has split churches and formed denominations. It is a difficult one because it goes to the heart of who we believe God is and how we view that precious gift of free will. Although this book is not meant to fully address this topic, it is a topic earnest Christians will explore. You will find a list of resources at www.directionanddiscernment.com to help you in your search for answers.

**Direction:** Below is a list of Scriptures to anchor your faith in that truth. Look up as many as your time allows.

Exodus 33:19               Deuteronomy 4:39

Psalm 29                    Isaiah 43:13

| | |
|---|---|
| Psalm 83:18 | Isaiah 44:24-28 |
| Psalm 135:5-6 | Daniel 4:34-35 |
| Proverbs 16:9 | John 19:10-11 |
| Isaiah 25:1 | Colossians 1:15-20 |
| Isaiah 37:26-29 | Revelations 1:8 |
| Isaiah 40:12-14 | Revelations 17:14 |

**Yield:** Spend your time of prayer praising the Sovereign Lord. Use the names in the index along with the scriptures you read to focus your communion on the Name above all other Names.

*Day Five*

**Stop:** As suggested on page 78, read the entire book of Esther without commentary or study notes.

Do you agree with the author (pg. 79) that the first part of verse 4:14 sums up the whole message of the Book of Esther? What is that message?

**Intersection:** Trust requires us to admit we are not _____ (pg. 79-80), and at the same time it allows us to participate in a story we cannot fully see. The author defines this as the "narrow way," and then goes on to say that working within God's sove-reign-ty is the hardest *and* easiest thing we will do.

Do you agree that "trust in God" is the narrow way?

What does she mean by sove-reign-ty?

How is placing your full trust in God the easiest and hardest thing you've ever done?

**Yield:** Praise God for sovereignly working to fulfill His purposes, carrying out His plan in cooperation with the choices you and I make. Ask God to help you walk the narrow way, to trust His mighty hand and outstretched arm.

GROUP STUDY
LESSON THREE

**Gathering Activity:** As people gather, explain that for the gathering activity they are to imagine their faith journey as a mountain climb. Invite them to choose one of the objects displayed on a table that best describes their climb up *Faith Mountain*. As they mingle, invite them to share why they chose their object. If you live near mountains and have access to these objects, by all means, use the real thing. An alternative is to download the picture list from www.directionanddiscernment.com, or simply print the object names and descriptions on index cards.

### Mountain Climbing Gear

| | |
|---|---|
| Anchoring devices | Water |
| Chalk/marking tags | Trail mix |
| Harness | Emergency flares |
| Backpack | Hiking/climbing shoes |
| Rope | Rain/snow gear |
| Weather/safety report | |
| Trail/climb map | |

**Opening Prayer:** Almighty and Sovereign God, we bow before you, the One True God. We know you have called us and brought us together to learn from Your Holy Word. We acknowledge our utter dependence upon Your Holy Spirit to guide us into all truth. We give You this time and pray that it be glorifying to You, even as Your Son, and the Spirit who now counsels us, glorifies You. In whose Name every knee shall bow, we offer this prayer. Amen.

**Stop:** Read 1 Kings, Chapter 17

**Background Information:** The king of Israel was Ahab who worshipped Baal, the pagan god of rain and harvest. Elijah was a reluctant prophet sent by God to warn Ahab and the Israelites that following Baal would not bring them what they needed— water. After delivering the message of the coming drought, God sends Elijah on a journey. However, this journey is not for the sake of the king or God's people; it was for Elijah.

**Discussion Questions:**

1. Elijah exhibited an enormous faith in blindly following God. In what ways was Elijah walking blind, and how were his steps more solid than some might think?

2. Three times Elijah's faith-walk, which at first appearance is rewarded with a good outcome, hits a rocky road and is even detoured. Some- times our faith-journey, although taking us right where God wants us to be, appears to hit rough patches and is sometimes derailed. What does Elijah's response tell us about our own faith-journeys? What does this tell us about God's sovereignty?

You would think that these were enough trials for Elijah, but the trials had not even begun. Chapter 18 tells the "big showdown story" between Ahab's god and Elijah's God. In a made-for-pique-drama scene, Elijah carries out his God's instructions, and with a ball of fire from heaven the Sovereign Lord declares His authority. Elijah stands tall upon the Rock, the foundation of God's sovereignty. But when Jezebel, Ahab's wife, threatens to kill him, Elijah's faith wanes. Pick up your reading of this story here.

**Stop:** Read 1 Kings Chapter 19:1-16

**Discussion Questions:**

1. How is it that the Elijah we saw earlier, the one who stood with the Lord against Ahab and his men, was now an emotional wreck?

2. When we take our eyes off the greatness of God, our weaknesses become magnified and the choices we must make become monumental (pg. 82). What does this say about faith, trust, worship, and God's call on our lives?

**Small Group Sharing:**

If your group is large, divide into groups of three or four. As a small group, reread verses 11 and 12. What does it mean to you for God to speak as a powerful wind, an earthquake, a fire, and finally, a gentle whisper?

God knew what Elijah needed at every step along His journey. God was not only working out His sovereign plan for the nation Israel, but He was also working in the heart of Elijah, shaping him into the man God created him to be. It is interesting to note that just because Elijah trusted God didn't mean he always felt close to Him, nor worthy of His calling. Elijah doubted, felt afraid, and became depressed. Yet, God spoke to him in his deepest need and used him mightily to accomplish His goals. For that we remember him, not only as one of the most famous prophets, but we also see him again in the appearance with Moses and Jesus on the Mount of Transfiguration. I'd say he learned to be a real mountaineer, wouldn't you?

After reading the story of Elijah, share your primary emotion with your group.

_____ overwhelmed at the idea of being called

_____ fear of being asked to do something that big

_____ peace because you see how God's sovereignty works

_____ inadequacy to the calling He's placing before you

_____ emboldened because you realize God is truly in control

**Yield:** Bring these emotions to the Lord in prayer. Ask Him to enter each person's life as a powerful wind, an earthquake, a fire, or a gentle whisper, whatever is needed in each situation. Close your time of prayer with each person praising God for His sovereign care for them and for those in your group.

# WEEK FOUR

**Directional "*signs*" in my week**

*Day One*

**Intersection:** The author says there are three things required for taking steps of faith. These steps are _____ , _____, and _____ (pg. 85). Do you find it is more difficult to summon courage, muster strength, or risk trusting?

**Discern:** Think about your childhood. Were you a compliant child who willingly followed the rules, or were you more of a rebellious nature, pushing the envelope of independence?

Now think about a time when you were put in a position of leadership. Did you find it easy to have others follow your lead? What about times you have been a follower: was it easy for you to accept someone else's lead, even if it meant limiting your own freedom?

How does our freedom-loving, free-spirited culture affect our view of freedom?

**Stop:** Read 1 Peter 2:16-17

If this is God's definition of freedom, how is this definition different from the definition used in our American culture?

Using the above Scripture, write your own definition of Christian freedom.

**Yield:** In prayer, ask God to forgive you for at times adopting the world's definition of freedom. Ask Him to help you live out this new definition of Christian freedom. Then ask Him to give you the courage and strength to walk in faith with trust in Him as the only true path to freedom.

*Day Two*

**Intersection:** In God's economy of freedom, self-centeredness is replaced by _____, our desire for no restraints with _____, and accountability only to self with_____, (pg. 87).

**Discern:** In the first rule of freedom, other-centeredness is the prescription for self-centeredness. How does becoming more other-centered free you?

The second requirement for God-given freedom is enslavement. How is enslavement a component of godly freedom?

Dying to self is the final key to unlocking genuine freedom. How is accountability a freeing thing in God's economy?

**Stop:** Read 2 Corinthians 3:17-18

Who is it that does the freeing?

If having "unveiled faces" means "laying open and uncovered," what does this imply we need to do in order to receive freedom?

**Decision:** Becoming "naked" before God by laying bare our souls is a difficult step for many of us. We often go to great lengths to hide our sins and the resulting shame, yet God tells us that only when we lay them bare will we be transformed from self-centered, chained-to-heavy-weights, accountable-to-no-one teens, to mature and free members of God's family. Are you being held prisoner by selfishness? Are you bound to peer approval, money and prestige, power and lust? Do you live your life accountable to no one but you? Freedom from that life of bondage is being offered to you. Are you willing to unmask yourself before Him?

**Yield:** In prayer, express your desire to be set free. Name those things that have bound you to other gods. As you become bare before the Lord, allow His love and forgiveness to transform you and to clothe you in righteousness. Ask God to help you walk in faith as one who has been transformed. Invite Him to continue to change you daily as you embrace this life of freedom.

*Day Three*

**Intersection:** Two Scriptural principles are at work in living out a life of freedom. The first one is the principle of _____(pg. 88).

The Narrow Way is also known as the _____ (Matthew 7:12).

This is the rule that governs the Kingdom of God, the second Scriptural principle at work in living out a life of freedom.

**Stop:** Read Matthew 6:33

**Discern:** If God's kingdom is the place where God's desires become tangible, where His desires become our own, how do the two Scriptural principles help us (pg. 89-90)? Hint: one is what we do or how we act, and the other is how we think.

**Decision:** When we pray, "Thy kingdom come," we invite God to transform our desires into His and we offer ourselves as instruments of kingdom-making here "on earth as it is in heaven." The Lord's Prayer is not a prayer asking God to magically make this world a place of peace and love. It is a prayer of sacrifice—our commitment of sacrificing our own selfish ways to those of the kingdom begun in us. How does this transform the way you will pray the Lord's Prayer from now on?

**Yield:** Pray using the Lord's Prayer, pausing and thinking about each phrase, offering your life to God as a kingdom-maker.

*Day Four*

**Intersection:** For faith to become an action-word, it must contain three components. Those components are:

1. Do _____,
   (pg. 90).

**Stop:** Look up Psalm 119:105 and see what the verses before it and after it are talking about. When the Psalmist refers to God's Word, what is he referencing?

What then does it mean to *do* what we already know?

    2. Do _____
       (pg. 90-91).

**Stop:** Look up Joshua 6:1-21, paying special attention to verse 10. Because a march is always followed by a war cry and then an attack, the warriors of Jericho would have been unnerved when the war cry didn't come and dismayed when the Israelites continued to march for five more days. Often what makes us stand apart is what attracts others to our faith. What other reasons could God have for asking us to follow this principle?

    3. Do _____
       (pg. 91).

**Stop:** Read Romans 12:10 and 1 Corinthians 10:23-24? How does the verse in Romans work alongside the verse in 1 Corinthians?

**Yield:** Ask God to help you "do" these things to take the concept of freedom in Christ from a cerebral thing to an action-word in your life. Tell God you want to not only be known as a man or woman of faith, but also as a man or woman of faith-action.

*Day Five*

**Intersection:** Yesterday we looked at three other-world faith steps in making faith an action-word. Today we'll look at the three this-world reactions to them (pg. 92-93).

1.  Doing _____.

2.  Doing _____.

3.  Doing _____.

**Discern:** Imagine you are a parent of a teenager who is giving you the above excuses to your rules of the "household of God." Using the information in the book, under each heading write out your response to your rebellious teen.

God must get a chuckle out of our rebellious teenager ways because, like us with our teens, He knows what it's like to be there. Although Christ never sinned, He lived with us in a human body and had teenage friends. He has watched teenagers behave this way since the beginning of time. He has also watched adults behave embarrassingly like teenagers. After all, does that not describe the nation Israel to a "t"? Just as we love our teens even if their behavior is anything but lovable, God loves us. He knows that growing up is hard and that one day we will thank Him for being a good and faithful parent.

**Yield:** In prayer, thank God for being a good and faithful parent, regardless of the temper tantrums and whining you've given Him. Ask Him to help you become less rebellious and more mature when the steps of faith become difficult. When the going gets tough and the tendency to slip back into "this-world reactions" comes, ask Him to help you remember you're a member of the "other-world."

GROUP STUDY
LESSON FOUR

**Gathering Activity:** Before your gathering, grab a pad of sticky notes and write messages to your group members of "incredible news they'd love to hear" such as "Joe, you've just won a million dollars from Publishers Clearing House," and "Mary, the IRS caught a mistake on last year's tax return and is refunding *you* nearly half of what you paid." As people gather, have them find their messages on the message board (a message center you can create from poster board or by using a small corkboard). This is a fun exercise in receiving messages that are "too good to be true."

**Opening Prayer:** Oh, Faithful and True God, we come before you as people of faith. We must admit, however, at times our faith is weak, and we sometimes act like rebellious teenagers complaining and whining about the *rules*. We know you have called us to be people of a different kingdom. Help us to become the people you've called us to be so others may come to know you as we do—a God who walks with us on this faith-journey and who takes all things and uses them for good. We pray this in the Spirit of the One who gives us faith. Amen.

**Weekly Review:** Discuss the week's lessons. What stood out for you in the reading or study? What questions did it create? What did you struggle with the most?

In this lesson, we will look at key passages in the story of Abraham (pg. 93-95), the great Patriarch of the Jewish nation. While we read together, may we each grow in our own understanding of what it means to walk by faith.

**Stop:** Read Genesis 12:1-4

**Discussion Questions:** Abram simply did as God told him, no questions asked. Up to this point, we have only learned of Abram through the description of his family.

1. Based upon your own faith history, would you say this event is early on in his faith journey?
2. What would you speculate was Abram's faith-history?
3. Do you think Abram's faith is a tested faith at this point?
4. Is this what is meant by childlike faith?

**Stop:** Read Genesis 12:7-9

**Discussion Question:** The Lord appeared to Abram again. This time, with a promise of land. It was common for altars to be built as a reminder of God's faithfulness, so Abram built an altar. Then he and his family lived in tents as aliens in a foreign land and they waited on God. God has made promises to you and me, promises to be with us through times of trial, to set us free from bondage, and to bring us joy unspeakable, and yet many of us are patiently waiting. Discuss what tie there might be between building an altar and waiting.

Stop: Read Genesis 16:1-16

**Discussion Question:** Abram grew tired of waiting. He, being led by his wife, devised a plan to fulfill God's promise. When you and I get tired of waiting on God, when we can't see His answers to our questions, we often choose to take matters into our own hands. Doing so always brings consequences. The jealousy between Sarah and Hagar would be transferred to their children, and their children's children. Even the tribes of Ishmael's descendants would be at war with one another. In spite of all of this, God was faithful to His promise. How does this story reflect your own experiences with taking matters into your own hands, and God's faithfulness despite your weakness?

Stop: Read Genesis 22:1-18

**Discussion Questions:** Years later, God told Abraham to take his only son up on a mountain and sacrifice him there on an altar he and his son will build. In a shift from his previous reactions, Abraham doesn't question God. He does exactly as God directs. Without knowing how God would make the situation right, Abraham trusted God to somehow fulfill His promises. There has been a noticeable growth in Abraham's faith. It appears he has returned to the same childlike faith that allowed him to simply trust and believe God when He first told him to pack up his family and set out on an unknown journey. What is the difference between that childlike faith and the faith we now see?

It's clear in this story that along the way Abraham made poor choices. When he needed to hold on to his faith and act accordingly, Abraham often failed. It is also clear that God was at work in Abraham's life, wooing him to choose wisely, and then intervening to make course corrections when Abraham's wrong choices could have derailed God's plans. Up until the final testing of his faith in the sacrifice of Isaac, Abraham's faith was tested in the laboratory of life—not by God. How then do we understand the phrase "tested faith is assured faith"?

How different might the story have been if God had "tested" Abraham before he was ready? How does it change your view of "the testing of faith" when you realize God had prepared Abraham for many years by walking with him as he made daily choices and therefore knew Abraham's faith would hold *before* the test was ever given? If God already knew what Abraham would do, why test him?

**Stop:** Read Hebrews 11:8-12, 17-34, 39-40 as preparation for prayer. Without interruption, after reading the Scripture say, "Let us pray."

**Yield:** Recite this prayer together from Hebrews 12:1-3:

Therefore, since we are surrounded by such a great cloud of witnesses, let us throw off everything that hinders and the sin that so easily entangles, and let us run with perseverance the race marked out for us. Let us fix our eyes on Jesus, the author and perfecter of our faith, who for the joy set before him endured the cross, scorning its shame, and sat down at the right hand of the throne of God. Consider him who endured such opposition from sinful men, so that you [and I] will not grow weary and lose heart. (NIV)

We ask in the Name of the Alpha and Omega, the beginning and end of our faith. Amen.

## WEEK FIVE

**Directional "*signs*" in my week**

*Day One*

**Stop:** Read Luke 5:33-39

**Discern:** The author makes the point (pg. 98-99) that just as Jesus knew change was difficult, we also find change hard. We struggle with our tendency to remain wrapped in our old and familiar ways. Mark below all the reasons you feel change is hard.

### <u>Reasons Change Is Difficult</u>

_____ the old is all I know

_____ the old is familiar and comfortable

_____ it's the way I was brought up

_____ it's the way it has always been

_____ what if I don't like the new

_____ it's too much effort

_____ it's hard work

_____ it might reveal more than I bargained for

_____ the unknown

_____ at least I knew the trouble spots with the old

_____ change has always brought pain

_____ I might have to make a sacrifice

_____ loss of control

_____ my motto is, if it ain't broken…

_____ my motto is, steady as she goes…

_____ change opens Pandora's box

_____ where's the catch

On a scale of 1-10, with 10 being "I fight it every step of the way" and 1 being "I welcome it," how would you rate yourself on your willingness to change?

**Direction:** In the Scripture reading, the Pharisees cannot accept Christ because their wineskins—the box that contained their views of Messiah and what was right and wrong—was too rigid. The fifth question, "Is it _____, _____, and _____ me?" is designed to confront us with this pharisaic tendency.

**Stop:** Read Genesis 37:5-11, and then Genesis 39:1-4.

**Discern:** A transformation has taken place and the only clue we have is found in Genesis 39:2. What does it mean by "the Lord was with Joseph"?

Was not God with Joseph from the beginning (pg. 101-102)?

The clue is in what we don't see. We don't see a cocky, braggart Joseph. In fact, we are told that all of the prosperity befalling Potiphar was because of the favor given Joseph by the Lord. But this time, we don't see Joseph bragging. When you and I spend time with the Lord, He isn't going to leave us where we are. He's going to change us. God wants to stretch, grow, and strengthen you and me for His glory.

**Yield:** In prayer, welcome God, the Change Agent, to have His will in your life. Share with Him your fears of change and then tell Him that out of obedience you're willing to change if He'll show you how.

*Day Two*

**Intersection:** God's exercise plan (pg. 102) includes _____ stiff necks, _____ proud knees, stretching us beyond the _____, growing within us an _____ of His ways, and strengthening our _____ in a bond of _____ and love.

The first step in the Exercise Plan is to learn how to distinguish God's voice from the voice of false gods (including ourselves). There are three distinguishing characteristics of God's voice:

1.  God speaks with authority (pg. 103)

**Stop:** Read Matthew 7:28-29. The religious leaders pointed to themselves using puffed up words and flowery language. How were Jesus' words different?

2.  God speaks with a gentleness of spirit (pg. 104)

**Stop:** Read John 20:10-16. Jesus could have appeared to Mary in a blazing light but instead He chose a Gardener. In that form, He still could have scolded her for her lack of faith, but instead He asked questions. Then He called her name. What other words do we use to describe this gentle spirit? Love? What else?

3.  God's voice is consistent with the content of His character (104)

**Stop:** Read Luke 24:13-32. The Risen Christ walked and taught the men along the road to Emmaus, but it wasn't until He broke the bread and gave thanks that the men's eyes were opened. Teaching, preaching, and even doing the right things doesn't always mean it is of God. There is something more. It must align with the character of God, which includes the power of the Holy Spirit. What other parts of God's character must be included in this assessment? Need a hint? Think of the Trinity.

**Yield:** In prayer, ask God to make His voice clear to you that you may recognize His voice apart from all others, including your own. End your time of prayer by simply sitting and listening in your thoughts or within your spirit. Just listen.

*Day Three*

**Intersection:** Spiritual discernment is *living* in an atmosphere of_____and_____in which one becomes keenly aware of the _____ _____of the Holy Spirit (pg. 106).

For the following, have in mind a decision you're contemplating, or one that you've recently made that caused you considerable angst. The more details you can hold in your mind about the situation and the emotions surrounding it, the more meaningful this exercise will be.

**Discern:** The three "occasions" for making wise and godly decisions are:

1. When _____ (pg. 107).

This first occasion is when God makes the choice clear, where there are no incongruencies between what you are contemplating and what God would be pleased with. If this is the case, then steps two and three are not needed.

2. When _____(pg. 107).

In contemplative prayer, consider the options before you. As you sift through those options in your mind, pay close attention to how your spirit reacts. Are there feelings of *consolation* where the Spirit is drawing you to that one choice and toward God, or are your feelings those of *desolation* with a focus that is moving away from God and more toward self?

3. When we need to go deeper in prayer because the answers are not clear.

For this step, you must find a place of peace and quiet. Spend some time quieting your spirit before centering your thoughts on the choices before you.

a. Begin by asking God, "Does this opportunity prevent or allow me to glorify You?" Wait and listen for an answer. Next, ask "Does it move me closer to my goal of becoming more Christlike?" Again, wait and listen for an answer. Many people choose to journal during this time, and if you wish to try this approach, be sure you've given ample time for reflective listening before writing.

b. The final step is a visualization exercise. During this step, you'll be looking for feelings of harmony or feelings of unrest. The idea here is that the Holy Spirit guides us into places of peace, harmony, and joy and uses feelings of unrest, confusion, and lifelessness to steer us away from things that aren't good choices. So, close your eyes.

- Imagine offering your decision to God. Wait…what do you feel?
- Picture advising someone else to make this decision. Wait…what do you feel?
- Suppose you've died and your decision is part of your eulogy. Wait…what do you feel?
- Envision yourself standing before the Judgment Seat of God; is this decision on your list of good or poor choices? Wait… what do you feel?

**Note:** If there is no clear choice one way or another, it may be that either choice is acceptable to God.

**Yield:** End your time of prayer thanking God for this time of communion with Him. If the answers are still not clear, ask God to continue to work in your thoughts and in your spirit. Praise Him for guiding you and walking with you as you make wise decisions.

*Day Four*

**Intersection:** The Wisdom Literature includes the books of _____, _____, _____, and _____ (pg. 110).

The book of Proverbs is an often-overlooked wealth of teaching on the foundational how-tos of applying wisdom to everyday life. Here is a framework for studying Proverbs and mining them for all they are worth:

Chapters 1-4 are written essay style and include an introduction on a disciplined life—a life of wisdom. (Key passages: 1:107, 2:6, 3:3-10)

Chapters 5-9 develop around two themes: adultery and the praise of true wisdom personified as a woman. (Key passages: 5:1-4, 21-23; 6:16-19; 20:23; 8:22-23)

Chapters 10-14 contrast the righteous and the wicked with more of a focus on specific acts. (Key passages: 10:19; 11: 2, 13-14, 22, 25; 12:1, 4, 14-16, 22-23; 13:12, 24; 14:1, 12, 23, 30-31)

Chapters 15-22 deal more with specific acts, and more for community and governance. Here we find the contrasts between the rich and the fool. (Key passages: 15:1, 18, 23, 32-33; 16:3, 9, 21, 24-25, 28, 32; 17:1, 9, 17, 22; 18:11-12; 19:8-9, 11, 20-21; 20:1, 5, 19; 21:2, 9, 13, 16, 23, 29; 22:2, 6, 11)

Chapters 22:17-24:22 are often called the "thirty sayings" of the wise and are general principles for living. (Key passages: 22:17-21; 23:13-14, 19-26, 29-35; 24:3-4, 17-18)

Chapters 25-29 focus on the three kinds of fools: the morally deficient, the obstinate, the perverse, or one who rejects God. This section deals more with the common life of everyday man. (Key passages: 25:7-10, 11-14, 21-22, 28; 26: 12, 21; 27: 3, 8, 15; 28:1, 9, 23, 26; 29:6, 7, 11, 20, 25)

Chapter 30 tells us God is the giver of wisdom; it cannot be earned or learned. The prayer in 30:7-9 and the list of objectionable persons 30:11-14 are of particular interest.

Chapter 31:10-31 is in praise of the virtuous woman.

**Yield:** Thank God for giving us this practical wisdom, and ask Him to help you apply what you read to the way you live your life.

*Day Five*

**Stop:** Read Proverbs 8:29-31 and John 1:1-3

**Discern:** Do you see the parallels between the personified wisdom in Proverbs and the Word Made Flesh in John (pg. 112-113)?

**Direction:** To plant all wisdom in our hearts, the author suggests using the Index Card Method. Choose two or three proverbs from yesterday's list to create your index cards. Place them around you throughout the day where you will see them repeatedly and will begin to memorize the words of wisdom.

**Intersection:** When the author describes the foundational Proverb to two of Jesus' famous teachings (Proverbs 25:6-8 for Luke 14:8-10; and Proverbs 24:3-4 for Matthew 7:24-27), do you see the connection?

**Yield:** Praise God for giving us true Wisdom in the life of Jesus Christ. Praise Him for being the foundation upon which we can build our faith, and ask Him to help you grow in that Wisdom.

## GROUP STUDY
## LESSON FIVE

**Gathering Activity:** Post a sign at the entrance for the gathering that says "God's Waiting Room." On a table, have slips of paper with one of the "options" below. To divide the group and determine how many of each option you'll need, divide the number of people in your group by four. Example: If you have nine in your group, have two index cards for each of three groups, and three for one.

### Options for "what they prefer to do in a waiting room."

- Read a magazine
- Text message or call a friend
- Catch up on work
- Clean out purse/wallet

**Opening Prayer:** God of New Wine, we come before you knowing we need to stretch and grow and change, but we must admit that at times it's difficult for us. We thank you for the testimony of Joseph, for in him we see a lot of our own weaknesses and are reminded that you still use broken vessels. We ask you to speak to us words of wisdom during our study as we diligently seek the leading of the Holy Spirit. Be with us now we ask in the name of the Wisdom we seek. Amen.

**Weekly Review:** Discuss the week's lessons. What stood out for you in the reading or study? What questions did it create? What did you struggle with the most?

**Discern:** Using the groups created in the opening activity (ex: the read a magazine group, and the catch up on work group), give each group ten to fifteen minutes to complete these assignments.

*Read a Magazine group*

You are hot-ace reporters and your instincts have led you to meet a man named Joseph at "Club Pharaoh" for a story on family reconciliation. You heard that Joseph had some unorthodox views on reconciliation, and so in preparation for this interview you've created a series of questions. You'll use Genesis 44:1-45:7 as your background material with 45:1-7 as your focus. You'll present this interview "live" to the rest of the group.

*Text Message or Call a Friend group*

Our ultimate Friend is God. Your group will write a text message or letter to God from Joseph that he might have sent at Genesis 43:30. Then write an answer from God. Genesis 42:18-43:30 are your background texts with 43:19-30 as your focus.

*Catch Up on Work group*

Joseph had a lot of time to meditate while he waited in his prison cell. You are Scribes in the

Temple and are busy recording the pithy wisdom given daily on the Temple broadcasts of WGOD Winning Ways AM. A prison guard has just come from Pharaoh's court seeking wisdom for a man who he says has been unjustly imprisoned there. The radio address today is to include sayings you are to write giving wisdom to this man. These new "Proverbs" will be read in the live radio address to be shared with the group. Use Proverbs 14:29 and 20:22 as a guide for the Proverbs, and Genesis 39 and 40 as your background.

*Clean Out Purse/Wallet group*

You are part of a large physicians' group in Egypt. Many people come to you for healing because your group practices many forms of natural and supernatural healing from ancient Israel. Each of you has a different specialty—personal and family systems counseling, anger management, forgiveness and spiritual healing, and behavior modification based upon ancient teachings. A man named Joseph has come to you asking for a prescription for what ails him. Each member of your team is to write him a script with detailed instructions on how to clean out his life, using your prescription. You'll use Genesis 41:1-42:28 as your background text.

**Small Group Sharing:**

The remainder of the time will be spent on the presentations from each group.

**Yield:** Close your gathering in prayer to a God who stretches, grows, and strengthens our faith. Praise Him for the spiritual muscles that were exercised during your gathering, and ask Him to be with each member this coming week.

**Directional "*signs*" in my week**

*Day One*

**Direction:** The sixth and final question: "Is this requiring me to _____, _____, and _____ my life (pg. 118)?

**Stop:** Read 1 Thessalonians 1:1-3:10

**Intersection:** It is obvious in the way this letter is written that Paul is addressing a list of questions he's received via a messenger. Although Paul tenderly and artfully tackles the issues of this young Christian congregation, it is clear through Paul's tone they have grown weary in well-doing while suffering persecution. It's no wonder they want to know "how long is this going to last?" Looking around our world at all the suffering, we too ask the same question.

**Discern:** Take time today to make a list of questions you have for God. These could be the "big theological questions" such as the ones we dealt with in the last chapter, or they could be more personal such as those that begin with "why...?"

## My Questions For God

**Yield:** In prayer, offer your questions to God. He is ready to listen. Then thank Him for always listening and for holding the answers to all questions in the palm of His hand.

*Day Two*

**Stop:** Read John 17:6-26

**Intersection:** The author defines sanctification (pg. 123) as "the way" to hold on until Christ's return. It's the process of being made holy, of returning us to that former state when we perfectly reflected the *Imago Dei,* where we simply knew God's ways. She also likens it to the process of salvation—not only saving us *from* sin, but *to* life abundant. The disciples must have had a million questions running through their heads as Jesus prayed this final prayer (pg. 121). In His divinity, He must have known each one, and yet these are the words He chose. Jesus chose to share with them His desire for them to be unified and sanctified. Think back to the Garden of Eden. How does "unity of spirit" and the concept of sanctification work together for our salvation?

**Discern:** Now look back at the list of questions you had for God yesterday. How does Jesus' answer of unity with your brothers and sisters in Christ and the process of sanctification and salvation answer those questions?

**Yield:** Thank Jesus that on the very night of His betrayal, He was thinking of you when He prayed for future believers. Express to Him your desire to learn how to walk in "the way."

*Day Three*

**Intersection:** Our part—adjustment—means to _____, to _____ to fit (pg. 123).

**Discern:** The author states that this first stage in the sanctification process is where most Christians are (pg. 124). Think back on your own faith journey. Do you recognize any of the early "sweet signs" of faith as ringing true in your life?

How about the tug-of-war, the battles with self-will, and the guilt (pg. 125)? Do these ring true in your experience?

**Stop:** Read Romans 7:14-19

**Decision:** As Paul so eloquently writes, we want control. We want to follow our own selfish desires, but at the same time we want to follow Christ. Are you tired of this war, or is there still some fight left within you?

The place of total surrender is also called consecration (pg. 125). To consecrate something is to initiate into service. This initiation is akin to the priestly ordination described in Leviticus.

**Stop:** Read Leviticus 8:1-12

The priests stood in the gap between man and God and were the overseers of the offerings. The anointing they received gave the priests the covering they needed to stand in God's presence on behalf of the Israelite nation. After Christ became our Chief Priest, we, His followers, were inaugurated into a new priestly tribe. No longer do we require an interface between God and us, but an offering was still needed—an offering of a fully surrendered heart. If the anointing oil in the priestly ordination described in Leviticus was an icon of the coming Holy Spirit, what does it mean for you and me to be *consecrated* in the process of sanctification?

**Yield:** In prayer, turn your attention to those "no trespassing" signs, hidden hallways, and closeted skeletons in your heart. If you're willing and ready, surrender these areas to God. In your mind's eye, take down the signs, turn on the light, and open the closed doors. Allow the anointing oil of the Holy Spirit to cover you in grace and love.

*Day Four*

**Discern:** John Wesley described the grace of God that goes before your acts of will as *prevenient* grace (pg. 126). In what ways has God's prevenient (anticipatory) grace been evident in your life?

The filling of the Holy Spirit with His life-transforming presence can happen at once at the time of conversion or as an event that happens *along* the journey, perhaps after a period of struggle. If you've experienced this in-filling, did it coincide with your conversion (like a Paul experience), or could you point to another time that followed an intense spiritual struggle for your filling—more like the disciples' experience (pg. 126-127)? Perhaps you have yet to experience this and are reading in hopes of learning how to receive this gift.

**Intersection:** The In-dwelling Holy Spirit does two things in the life of the believer:

1. First, the Holy Spirit comes to _____ (pg. 126).
   After reading the author's description of this step, describe this process in your own words.

2. Second, the Holy Spirit comes as _____ _____ to perfect (pg. 127). Likewise, describe this step of the process. How are the Tongues of Fire a good metaphor?

**Stop:** It takes both the purifying effect of the baptism (John 1:5) and the perfecting work of the Refiner's Fire (Malachi 3:2) to allow our wills to operate in harmony with God's.

**Yield:** Imagine yourself as a child running to God with a clump of fading and wilted flowers in your hands. Those flowers were picked from the garden of your heart. At the time of picking, they looked lovely. In the light of His presence, you see them as they really are, clumped with weeds of discontent and selfish ambition. Somehow you manage to offer these—the only gifts you have to offer—to your Heavenly Father, who takes them into His hand. As He does, they are transformed into the most beautiful flowers you've ever laid eyes upon. And God smiles at you.

*Day Five*

**Intersection:** Of the three analogies—the hand-me-down clothes, the bridge and truss work, or character education versus integrity education—which one best describes for you the process of growing in grace or realigning (pg. 128-129)?

At several points in this study, we've heard of the need for unity of spirit. Here, we learn the reason. The goal of the Change Agent is to transform us into people of integrity. Using the clothing, building, or education analogy, how would you describe this final step?

**Discern:** If God replaces our weaknesses with His strengths, how does He "fill out" (clothing analogy) our clothes with His righteousness, add support beams (building analogy) to our trusses, or overcome our selfish tendencies (education analogy)?

**Stop:** Read Philippians 3:12-14

Christian perfection (pg. 130) is different from worldly perfection in that worldly perfection is about outward behavior. Christian perfection is found in the intent of the heart. It is about the destination our vessel is charted toward, the orientation of our focus, or the chalk-line used to guide our life's construction. How does this understanding set us free from the "tyranny of having to know God's will," to *resting* in God *as* His will?

**Yield:** In prayer, offer God your weaknesses, inviting Him to be seen through them rather than you striving to hide or fix them. Thank God that Christian perfection is about *becoming* rather than *being* perfect. Ask Him to help you make "resting in Him" your goal.

GROUP STUDY
LESSON SIX

**Gathering Activity:** If you have hymnals available, provide one for each person. You may also find the words to the songs on the Internet. As a gathering activity, have people share with others how music has ministered to them or how it has shaped their faith. You may want to have music playing in the background to set the mood. Choose the music type that will best fit your group—gospel, classic hymns, instrumental, organ, or perhaps early contemporary Christian.

**Opening Prayer:** Lord, we thank you that you have brought us together once again. We thank you for the many ways you have paved the way for us to be where we are with you today. We also thank you for the ways music has played a big or small part in the shaping of our faith. May we continue to grow in the grace of your love as we study together. We ask in the Name of the One from Whom all blessings flow.

Sing together the doxology:

> Praise God from whom all blessings flow;
>
> Praise Him, all creatures here below;
>
> Praise Him above, ye heavenly host;
>
> Praise Father, Son, and Holy Ghost. Amen.

**Weekly Review:** Discuss the week's lessons. What stood out for you in the reading or study? What questions did it create? What did you struggle with the most?

**Discussion Questions:** Review the ending portion of Chapter Six under the subtitle "God's Will" (pg. 130).

1. What thoughts, phrases, sentences jumped out for you?
2. What new insights did you receive?
3. How does this redefine "maturity" and "perfection" for you?
4. Can you put "God's Way" into a two- or three-sentence definition?

Whether you're from an emerging worship church, or you are a traditional or blended worship congregation, we can all learn from the classic hymns. Hymns were the "people's way" of learning the basics of the Christian faith, the tenets of orthodox Christianity, if you will. Set to music, these lessons were easy to memorize and to keep with the people during trials or hardships. Hymns were also available to those who could not read or attend worship. Today, hymns bring many back to their childhood, and for some, hymns are a new treasure trove of unexplored riches.

**Small Group Activity:** You may wish to do this as a group or divide into smaller groups of four or five people. Explore the hymns listed below. First, read through the lyrics. Is there a pattern, a theme? What tenets of the faith is this hymn teaching? What do you find meaningful, beautiful? Now, if possible listen to the song. How does the melody capture the message? If you so choose, sing the final verse. Allow the message and melody to speak to your spirit.

For copyright reasons, I haven't reprinted the hymns here but hope you have hymnals or at least access to the Internet (www.cyberhymnal.org and www.hymnsite.com are two of my favorites; you can also reach these through my Web site, www. directionanddiscernment.com) where you can find the lyrics, sheet music, even MIDI files so you can hear the hymns.

Have Thine Own Way, Lord*
Take My Life and Let It Be*
Take Time to Be Holy*
Holy Spirit, Faithful Guide
Just As I Am*
True-Hearted, Whole-Hearted*
Jesus, Savior, Pilot Me
Love Divine, All Loves Excelling*
O for a Heart To Praise My God*

*If time is limited or if you wish to do this exercise as a group, choose these songs.

**Yield:** For a closing prayer, light a Christ (white) candle to signify the Light in your presence and sing together the Christmas hymn "Away In A Manger." Be sure to sing the third verse (pg. 132).

**Directional "*signs*" in my week**

*Day One*

**Discern:** In your natural personality, do you tend to be more goal oriented or process oriented?

**Intersection:** This chapter gives six obstacles to hearing from God. What is the first obstacle listed (pg. 133)?

God's goal is both

- I _____ in that He wants to redeem _____ of us, including _____ _____ (pg. 133). Define this in your own words.

- C _____ in that He wants to redeem those parts of our lives that _____, and this includes our relationships with _____ _____ (pg. 134). Define this in your own words.

**Direction:** So, what do we do while we wait? We follow the principle summed up in the following phrase.

> Joy is found in the journey,
> not in the destination.

Put a checkmark next to they activities you routinely engage in, and a circle around those you plan to incorporate more fully in your life.

_____ Celebrate each victory over sin.

_____ Rejoice when I've turned one more area over to God for redemption.

_____ Rest in God's promises to never leave me or forsake me.

_____ Relax, knowing God is not finished with me yet.

List other ways you've found to "enjoy the journey." _____

**Yield:** As you come before God in prayer, remember He made you the way you are as either a goal or process-oriented person. Ask Him to work within that God-given personality to help you learn how to stay focused on the journey with Him as well as on the destination.

*Day Two*

**Intersection:** The next obstacle given is _____ _____ (pg. 135).

How does the phrase "Pigs don't know when pigs stink" characterize our relationship to sin and forgiveness?

**Discern:** Place a checkmark next to all of the areas of forgiveness you find difficult.

I struggle with forgiveness in the following areas...

_____ applying it only to those who've asked, repented, or who I feel deserve it

_____ whitewashing my own sin while spotlighting others'

_____ neglecting our corporate sin while only focusing on personal sin

_____ believing that forgiveness is a feeling I must have before offering it

_____ believing it is a one-time thing and not realizing the many layers in the process

_____ refusing to recognize my need for further forgiveness as I allow wounds to fester

_____ becoming hard of heart by holding onto unforgiveness

_____ not separating forgiveness (an act of obedience) from forgetting (God's role)

**Direction:** Satan doesn't want us to have victory in forgiveness. He wants to convince us we haven't done it right and that we are unworthy of true forgiveness. Or he wants us to believe our sins are outside of God's power of forgiveness. How does Satan use our memories to accomplish this goal (pg. 136-137)?

How should we react when Satan reminds us of past sins?

**Yield:** Spend your prayer time talking with God about forgiveness. Review with Him the areas of struggle you marked in the list above. Remember to seek forgiveness for both corporate and personal sins. Then ask God to help you cling to His grace all the more when memories of past sinfulness come back to distract you.

*Day Three*

**Intersection:** The third obstacle in hearing from God is _____of _____ because it can prejudice the communication (pg. 137).

We prevent this by learning the language He is speaking, not the one we want to impose.

**Discern:** The following scriptures are often used to support the *Personal Pathways* language, but the author is giving an alternative view. Describe both views for each of the passages.

* **Stop:** Read Proverbs 16:9 (pg. 138)

  Personal Pathways:

  Alternative View:

* **Stop:** Read Romans 12:1-2 (pg. 139)

  Personal Pathways:

  Alternative View:

* **Stop:** Read Ephesians 2:10 (pg. 140)

  Personal Pathways:

  Alternative View:

**Direction:** The Greek word for "the will" is *gevlhma*, which actually means God's desires, His wishes, dreams, or pleasures. Insert these words into the above passages instead of the word "will." How does this change your interpretation of these?

**Yield:** Ask God to forgive you if you've either willingly or unknowingly imposed a language or interpretation upon His words. Ask Him to help you remove the filter that you've placed there so you may clearly see His words as He meant them to be heard.

*Day Four*

**Intersection:** The next obstacle to hearing from God is defined as _____ of _____, which is defined as a body of _____ (pg. 141).

**Stop:** Read 1 Corinthians 12:14-19, and then read the introduction to this section 12:1-3.

**Discern:** Here, God's voice is set in contrast to _____ idols. These idols are not "not speaking," as the next verse tells us. Rather they are speaking without the power of truth. As we've already discussed, one of the biggest idols we struggle with is self—being self-sufficient, self-reliant, and self-absorbed. Community combats this tendency to self-focus by focusing us on the Christ in others. It is in others that we begin to hear the richness of His voice. How are you involved in hearing God through community?

**Decision:** In the index, review the steps for using a Community of Faith in decision-making. Who might you include as potential members of your *Clearness Committee*?

### People I might ask to be on my Clearness Committee

**Yield:** In prayer, ask God to reveal to you those who might serve well on your Clearness Committee. Ask Him to forgive you for falling into the trap of viewing "hearing from Him" as only a personal activity. And then thank Him for making His voice heard more clearly through the gift of community.

*Day Five*

**Intersection:** The fifth obstacle to hearing God's voice is too many _____ and too many _____ (pg. 144).

**Discern:** Do you agree or disagree that having too may choices can lead us into believing we are in control?

Do you see how *choice* can become an addiction (pg. 145)?

**Intersection:** Because of this addiction, we have made choice our _____ by emotionally connecting to those choices. To manage our addiction, we must _____ ourselves from the need to control things (pg. 145).

As of way of acknowledging your desire to divorce from the need for choice, use the following Divorce Degree.

*Divorce Decree*

I, _____, acknowledge my need for many choices. I understand that the feelings of empowerment I receive when given so many choices, or the negative feelings of choice-overload, are signals that my addiction to choice has placed choice in the position of god. I know you are a jealous God. I, therefore, pledge to place you center-stage in my life, and not my need to control things through the managing of the many choices. I hereby pledge my allegiance to You, Father God, and hereby sign this divorce decree on _____(date).

_____
Your Signature

**Yield:** Now make this pledge complete by taking it to the Lord in prayer. Ask Him to remind you of this pledge whenever the need for choice threatens to become an idol.

## Group Study
## Lesson Seven

**Gathering Activity:** Make enough copies of the "Spiritual/Biblical Literacy Test" from Appendix B for every member of the group. Hand each person a pencil or pen and a Spiritual/Biblical Literacy Test when they arrive, and have them complete it. Be certain to tell everyone this test is meant to be fun.

**Opening Prayer:** We praise you, O God, for not only hearing our prayers, but also for being a God who speaks to us. We're sorry we haven't heard your voice, that we have wanted our own ways, and have at times placed other things on the throne of our lives. Help us to hear you now as we gather. We ask this in the name of the God who created the universe with just one Word. Amen.

**Weekly Review:** Discuss the week's lessons. Which of the obstacles to hearing from God did you have the most trouble identifying with? What did you find the most helpful? Where did you have questions? What did you "take away" from this week's reading and study?

**Group Discussion:** Although the Spiritual/Biblical Literacy Test was just for fun, the statistics quoted by Barna show that Spiritual and biblical illiteracy, even among Bible study-attending, church going believers, is no laughing matter (pg. 146). This would be a good time to discuss what your church or community offers in the form of comprehensive Bible study (see www.directionanddiscernment.com for a list of good studies) and what your group plans to do next. For the majority of your lesson time, walk through Chapter seven, asking if the group members agree with the author and, if they do, how reading this chapter has helped them to mitigate this obstacles effectiveness.

The reason we don't want to receive God's word only in bite-sized pieces (pg. 148) is that we run the risk of developing a disjointed view of God, disconnecting His actions from the overarching story of who God is—His purposes and ours. When this occurs we cannot fully live out *our* story (both as individuals and as a part of the body), which can only be fully comprehended as a part of the greater story—*His* story.

**Group Exercise:** As an exercise in "story," copy on different colored paper the two lists from the back of this book ("Elements of a Story" parts A and B) and cut them apart before the meeting. The task of the group is to match the one set of "elements" to its corresponding "element" of a different color. Then, put them in story order (an answer key is given in Appendix C).

**Group Discussion:** How does knowing that your own story is part of a larger story—your community of faith's story, the story of the body of believers around the world, the story of the faith-filled throughout history, and the Greatest Story Ever Told—affect how you live out your life? Does it change anything?

**Yield:** Close by remaining in silent prayer following the reading of the paraphrase of Matthew 5:14-16 found at the end of Chapter Seven. Remain in silent prayer as the message of the words and the lessons stirred in this group lesson permeates your minds, giving God opportunity to speak within that silence.

**Directional "*signs*" in my week**

*Day One*

**Intersection:** The four guideposts (pg. 153) in the "Personal Pathways Approach to Spiritual Discernment" are:

1. _____

2. _____

3. _____

4. _____

**Discern:** The difference in the Personal Pathways Approach and the Wisdom Way is not in the guideposts, but in the _____ in reading those signs (pg. 153). Explain.

The intent of reading road signs in the Wisdom Way is to grow in wisdom—not find an individual will. Does this sound unsettling to you, or do you sense some truth in it?

**Yield:** In prayer, share with God your fears about trying a new way. Then ask Him to help you keep an open mind until all the evidence is in, and then to give you the courage to step through the open door if it is indeed a door for you.

*Day Two:*

**Stop:** Read Romans 1:8-13

> First, I thank my God through Jesus Christ for all of you, because your faith is proclaimed throughout the world. For God, whom I serve with my spirit by announcing the gospel of his Son, is my witness that without ceasing I remember you always in my prayers, asking that by God's will I may somehow at last succeed in coming to you. For I am longing to see you so that I may share with you some spiritual gift to strengthen you—or rather so that we may be mutually encouraged by each other's faith, both yours and mine. I want you to know, brothers and sisters, that I have often intended to come to you (but thus far have been prevented), in order that I may reap some harvest among you as I have among the rest of the Gentiles. NRSV

**Intersection:** As you read along in the chapter, use these markings to label the significant benchmarks in Romans 1:8-13 (pg. 155):

- Place a question mark above the word "prayer" identifying it at the guidepost Paul used.

- Underline "by God's will" to denote how this would be accomplished.

- Put an exclamation mark over "what Paul was hoping to be able to do."

- Put a number 1, and then a number 2 over the two reasons Paul gives for believing this was a wise decision.

- Again, underline "why he has not been able to complete his mission before."

- Finally, circle what reason Paul attributes to God's sovereign act in preventing him from following through on his commitment.

**Direction:** Here are the things we can glean from Paul's use of the Wisdom Way: use the book to define Paul's use of each question. The first and last ones have been completed for you.

1. Is this aligned with the character of God (pg. 155)?
   Paul knew God well enough to know this decision was within the boundaries of God's character.

2. Is there an obstacle or opposition (pg. 156)?

3. Is it God-sized?

4. Is it requiring steps of faith?

5. Is it stretching, growing, and strengthening you?

6. Is it requiring me to adjust, prune, and realign my life?

   This is evidenced in the whole process, for Paul was required to constantly adjust, prune, and realign his life in order to fulfill his calling.

**Yield:** Thank God for the witness He gave you and me in the life of the Apostle Paul. Ask Him to help you to be as obedient as Paul, willing to walk in the Ways of Wisdom.

*Day Three*

**Stop:** Read Colossians 4:3 and insert the words "of opportunity" after the words "open to us a door" as you read.

**Stop:** Read 1 Corinthians 16:7-9

Note that Paul is not seeking to know God's will, but only submitting His plans to the sovereign hand of God (pg. 156). And once again, we see the door of opportunity analogy used. This time Paul has decided to stay in Ephesus because a door of opportunity has been made available—not that the open door was pointing him to discern God's plan.

**Stop:** Read 2 Corinthians 2:12-13

If an open door is to be used by Christ's followers as a sign directing us to discern His will, then Paul's dismissal of this "sign" would be depicted in Scripture as an affront to God (pg. 157). It is not; by contrast, it is merely depicted as an opportunity, possibly among many, to which wisdom should be applied.

**Intersection:** By studying the Word of God, we learn what is clear in the Scriptures so we know when to choose one option over another. Then, where there is no clear leading, God expects us to use wisdom to walk in _____.

When we know God walks with us no matter _____ we choose, we experience _____ in knowing God will fulfill His purposes _____ (pg. 158). That is the key!

**Yield:** Express your desire to make decisions with Him, using the Ways of Wisdom as Paul did. Praise Him for being a God who takes our decisions, whether poorly or wisely chosen, and works them all for good.

*Day Four*

**In Review:**

All of what we need to know of God's will is clearly revealed in Scripture.

1. Through the stories and the overarching story of the Bible, we learn to walk by faith and trust in God's goodness (questions two and four).
2. As we study and apply His word, we check our motives (question three),
3. build spiritual muscles (question five),
4. and develop holiness of heart and hand, becoming and doing God's will here as it is in heaven (question six).

**Discern:** As you revisit the stories of Marcie, Torrie, Wendy, and James (pg. 159-160), ask yourself how the Wisdom Way versus the Personal Pathways Approach may have saved them some grief, and how their stories have been changed with the application of Wisdom's Ways. Which one of the stories most clearly speaks to you? How does their application of the Wisdom Way apply to your own decision-making?

**Yield:** Thank God for making His way clear when that way is the only way. Express your gratitude for a God who trusts you and me to make wise decisions when the way is not absolute—when the Wisdom Way is to be applied. Ask God to help you grow in your faith as you seek to apply this new Wisdom Way just as Marcie, Torrie, Wendy, and James did.

*Day Five*

**Intersection:** As you read "The Rest of the Story" (pg. 161), think about your own story. How has God woven your story into His? How have you seen the sovereign hand of God moving in your life, taking the decisions you've made and working them together for good?

**Final Exercise:** In preparation for your final group gathering, write a single-page retelling of your story. Use the Elements of Story used in the last group gathering as a guide (see Appendix A). The beginning of your story might not be at your birth (the author's own story began with a crisis of faith). It may be more of a slice of life story. Think

*Guideposts* or *Chicken Soup*-type stories in which you will show your own faith crises or stumbles, and God's faithfulness. Bring this story with you to the next gathering.

**Yield:** Praise God for how He has been faithful in your life. Ask Him to give you the courage to share your story as a testament to Him so others may come to know Him as you do.

## Group Study
## Lesson Eight

**Gathering Activity:** Have a stone or a rock for each member of your group. As group members arrive, be sure they have their written story, and then hand them a rock to place together with other members' rocks to build an "Altar to God's Faithfulness." You may want to add votive candles to your altar before you gather for prayer.

**Opening Prayer:** Light the candles and together read Psalm 111.

> Praise the LORD.
> I will extol the LORD with all my heart
> in the council of the upright and in the assembly.
> Great are the works of the LORD;
> they are pondered by all who delight in them.
> Glorious and majestic are his deeds,
> and his righteousness endures forever.
> He has caused his wonders to be remembered;
> the LORD is gracious and compassionate.
> He provides food for those who fear him;
> he remembers his covenant forever.
> He has shown his people the power of his works,
> giving them the lands of other nations.
> The works of his hands are faithful and just;

all his precepts are trustworthy.
They are steadfast forever and ever,
done in faithfulness and uprightness.
He provided redemption for his people;
he ordained his covenant forever—
holy and awesome is his name.
The fear of the LORD is the beginning of wisdom;
all who follow his precepts have good understanding. To Him belongs eternal praise. (NIV)

**Weekly Review:** Discuss the week's lessons and the impact this study and the book has had on your life. In what ways have you been challenged? How has your faith-walk been strengthened? Is the six-question decision-making method (God's Way or Wisdom Way) something you intend to incorporate into your life? How can we as a group support you in your goals?

**Group Sharing:** This is to be a sacred time, as members of your group share their personal and intimate stories of faith. For some it may be the first time they have ever shared their testimony, so be mindful of this and set the tone as you introduce this sharing time. Invite each person to read his or her own story of God's faithfulness. As each member finishes their story, use the response from Psalm 136—"His love endures forever"—as a group response to the testimony. Your group may choose to also share words of encouragement and support following each reading and the response.

**Yield:** Thank your group members for a wonderful experience. Remind them of the first meeting and the promise that was made from Jeremiah 17:7-8 (you may wish to read this again) and how you just witnessed that promise lived out in the testimonies that were read. As a closing, you may choose to sing the contemporary Christian song, "Forever" by Delirious, or to read responsively Psalm 136, which is titled "the never-ending story of God's love."

# APPENDIX A

## ELEMENTS OF A STORY, PART A

| Beginning | Middle | End |
|---|---|---|
| Plot/Action | Crisis/Climax | Conflict/Problem |
| Resolution | Characters | Moral/Message |

## ELEMENTS OF A STORY, PART B

| | | |
|---|---|---|
| Covenant, rejection, renewal of covenant, rejection, new covenant, rejection, covenant kept | The Suffering Messiah/The Christ Event | Shalom—unity/ Sin—separation |
| New Heaven and a New Earth | The Holy Trinity/Creator and the created | Paradise lost/ Paradise restored |
| For God so loved the world… | The Word/Let us make them in our image | His faithfulness endures |

# APPENDIX B

### A Spiritual/Biblical Literacy Test

Mark one answer for each question below. Next, check your answers with the key (no cheating now—we *are* Christians ☺) and then transfer your score to the rating's chart. Good luck!

1.  Which of these phrases from the Lord's Prayer are not in the Bible?

    A.  Our Father, in heaven
    B.  On earth as it is in heaven
    C.  And lead us not into temptation
    D.  For Thine is the kingdom and the power and the glory forever. Amen.

2.  Who were the only two people to have never died?
    A.  Moses and Enoch

B. Enoch and Elijah

C. Elisha and Moses

D. Lazarus and Moses

3. A model friendship grew between King David and what other biblical character?
   A. Goliath       C. Jonathan
   B. Saul          D. Bathsheba

4. Who was *not* one of the twelve disciples of Jesus?
   A. Matthew       C. Bartholomew
   B. Andrew        D. Luke

5. Which name is not one of the books of the Old Testament?
   A. Ezra          C. Amos
   B. Haggai        D. Onesimus

6. Which of the following beliefs isn't included in the Apostles' Creed as a foundational belief of the church?
   A. Jesus Christ was God's only son
   B. God is both "God the Father" and the "Maker of Heaven and Earth"
   C. Jesus was crucified by the Jews and was buried
   D. On the third day Christ arose

7. Where did Jesus' first miracle take place?
   A. During a storm at sea
   B. In a field with 5,000 men
   C. At a wedding party
   D. When teaching about being "fishers of men"

8. In the parables of the Lost Sheep, Lost Coin, and Lost Son, what was Jesus teaching about?
   A. Finding our way back to the Lord
   B. God's love persistently seeks, waits, and then rejoices over the lost when found
   C. How we are to persistently look for God because we are lost sinners
   D. Seeking and knocking on the door of God's heart

9. What is a "Harmony of the Gospels"?
   A. Matthew, Mark, Luke, and John blended into one account in chronological order.
   B. A list of those passages that can be "proven" because they are in all four gospels.
   C. A list showing where there are no contradictions between Matthew, Mark, Luke, and John.
   D. A resource book, like a concordance, that shows all the scriptures that talk about love, unity, brotherhood, sharing, and peace.

10. Who was the writer of over half the books in the New Testament?
    A. Luke          C. John
    B. Peter         D. Paul

    The last five questions are true/false. You have a fifty/fifty chance with these.

11. All Christian denominations can trace their heritage back through the Catholic Church.
    True            False

12. Psalms is often called the Hebrew Song Book.
    True                False

13. The term "New Testament" simply means "new covenant."
    True                False

14. The "apocrypha" is a collection of heretical books with no biblical value.
    True                False

15. The prophet most often quoted at Christmas is Jeremiah.
    True                False

## Ratings Chart

13 or more correct
_____ Congratulations! You are biblically and spiritually literate. Keep growing.

10-12 correct
_____ You've done well, but a few more Bible studies or spiritual formation classes wouldn't hurt. Keep up the good work!

9 or fewer correct
_____You may want to sign up for the next Bible study or spiritual formation retreat. However, your willingness to take this test proves you've got what it takes—now go for it!

**Test Key:** 1 D, 2 B, 3 C, 4 D, 5 D, 6 C, 7 C, 8 B, 9 A, 10 D, 11 T, 12 T, 13 T, 14 F, 15 F

# APPENDIX C

### ANSWER KEY FOR ELEMENTS OF A STORY

Here are the pairings, in order:

Beginning: The Word/Let us make them in our image

Characters: The Holy Trinity/Creator and the created

Conflict/Problem: Shalom—unity/Sin—separation

Plot/Action: Covenant, rejection, renewal of covenant, rejection, new covenant…

Middle: His faithfulness endures

Crisis/Climax: The Suffering Messiah/The Christ Event

Resolution: Paradise lost/Paradise restored

End: New Heaven and a New Earth

Moral/Message: "For God so loved the world…"

### Resources Needed For Each Group Lesson

For each lesson, you'll want to have extra Bibles for those who don't have their own or have forgotten to bring their own. You'll also want to provide nametags and pencils or pens. For the first lesson, be sure to have enough workbooks and books for each person who didn't already pick theirs up prior to the introductory class.

Reminder: there are many downloadable resources at www.directionanddiscernment.com. The items marked * are available there for your convenience.

**Introductory Class**

- Basket of apples and oranges
- Sign that reads Jeremiah 17:7-8*
- Slips of paper with the fruit names—apples, oranges, grapes, peaches
- If using the alternative game: a hula hoop and a beanbag for each person*
- Index cards

**Group Lesson One**

- Special nametags with the words, "I See God As…"*

### Group Lesson Two

- Solid color bathrobe or sheet with a rope belt
- Another sheet
- A hat or sunglasses
- A scroll—tape together several sheets of paper and roll like a scroll
- A feather pen—can be a pen with a feather taped to it

### Group Lesson Three

- Mountain-climbing objects—the real things or pictures of the objects,* or simply write the names of the objects on index cards

  Anchoring devices

  Chalk/marking tags

  Harness

  Backpack

  Rope

  Weather/safety report

  Trail/climb map

  Water

  Trail mix

  Emergency flares

  Hiking/climbing shoes

  Rain/snow gear

## Group Lesson Four

- Pad or sticky notes or a memo pad with "too good to be true" notes written to each person in the group
- A message center created from a posterboard, or use a small corkboard

## Group Lesson Five

- "God's Waiting Room" sign*
- Slips of paper with waiting room options*:
  Read a magazine
  Text message or call a friend
  Catch up on work
  Clean out purse/wallet
- Eight to ten sheets of blank paper or a legal pad

## Group Lesson Six

- A hymnal for every person or lyric sheets downloaded from Web sites listed in the lesson
- Recordings of hymns
- A Christ candle—a white pillar candle
- Matches or lighter

## Group Lesson Seven

- Copies of Appendix B*

- Copies of Appendix A*, Part A on one color of paper, and copies of Part B on another color of paper; then cut them apart

**Group Lesson Eight**

- A stone or rock for each person
- Votive candles
- Matches or lighter

Cheri is available for retreats and day-seminars.

Her *Hello God, Is This Really You* seminar and retreats formed the basis for this book and the study. In addition to this presentation, Cheri has added two more, *Mountain Climbing 101: Having Faith that Moves Mountains,* and *Running the Obstacle Course: Six Obstacles to Hearing from God.*

To schedule Cheri for your upcoming speaking needs, visit her Web site, www.CheriCowell.com, or link through www.directionanddiscernment.com, or call her at 407-366-6863 (Eastern Time).

# ABOUT THE AUTHOR

Cheri Cowell, a popular conference speaker and author, writes and speaks on the topics of spiritual growth and discipleship. Her much-requested *Hello God, Is This Really You* seminars and retreats formed the basis for her book, *Direction: Discernment for the Decisions of Your Life* (Beacon Hill, 2007), and the accompanying workbook Bible study, *Direction: A Companion Workbook for Practicing the Process of Discernment* (Pleasant Word, 2008). Currently, Cheri attends Asbury theological seminary (Orlando) where she is seeking an MA in theological studies. Cheri draws upon this, as well as her fifteen years of professional and lay ministry, to speak to the needs of Christians looking for "answers to the unspoken questions of faith." Cheri and her husband, Randy, call Orlando, Florida, home.